First World W

and Army of Occupation
War Diary
France, Belgium and Germany

9 DIVISION
1 Lowland Brigades
King's Own Scottish Borderers
5th Battalion.
1 April 1919 - 31 August 1919

WO95/1776/4

The Naval & Military Press Ltd
www.nmarchive.com
Published in association with The National Archives

Published by

The Naval & Military Press Ltd

Unit 10 Ridgewood Industrial Park,

Uckfield, East Sussex,

TN22 5QE England

Tel: +44 (0) 1825 749494

www.naval-military-press.com

www.nmarchive.com

Contents

LOWLOND (LATE 9) DIV

1 LOWLAND BRIGADE

5 BN. K.O.S.B

1919 APR — 1919 AUG

(from 34 DIV 103 BDE)

Appendix to War Diary.

	Officers	O.R.
Effective Strength at 31/3/19,..................	65.	855.
Number sick, invalided, and transferred.	2.	26.
Number of men Demobilised.	17.	250.
Reinforcements Received during month	11.	-
Effevtive Strength 30/4/19,,,,,,,,,............,;	57.	579.

From

C. Connell. Lieut- Colonel,

Comdg 5th Bn The Kin s Own Scotish Borderers

1/5/19.

HEADQUARTERS,
1st INFANTRY BDE.,
LOWLAND DIVISION.

No. BM/....../2.

Date.. 1/5/19.

Vol 13

Army Form C. 2118.

WAR DIARY
or
INTELLIGENCE SUMMARY.

(Erase heading not required.)

Instructions regarding War Diaries and Intelligence Summaries are contained in F. S. Regs., Part II. and the Staff Manual respectively. Title pages will be prepared in manuscript.

Place	Date	Hour	Summary of Events and Information	Remarks and references to Appendices
SOLINGEN	Apr 1	1430	Training according to Programme. (Indoor training for A & B Coys) Lecture in Kinosaal on "Advantages of enlisting in the Post-Bellum Army"	(note)
	Apr 2		Training according to Programme.	
	Apr 3		Training as per Programme.	
	Apr 4		Training as per Programme. Major R.N.S. Paton D.S.O. M.C. assumes command on Lt. Col. Curtis Hand D.S.O. evacuated sick. Coys 4	
	Apr 5		Training as per Programme	
	Apr 6		Church parade. Presbyterian 1030; C. of E. 0930; R.C. 1015	
	Apr 7	0900	Coys Parade in competition	
		0940	Pioneer Parade in Germerann yard	
		1600	Battalion Training School for junior officers, N.C.O.'s relieve private commander of Battalion proceeded to field near RANNENHOF for training	
	Apr 8		Parade etc. as yesterday	
	Apr 9		Training as per programme	
	Apr 10		Training as per programme	
	Apr 11		Training as per programme. Both for A.C.D Coys	
		1130	Lecture in Kinosaal by Rev. S.H. Kendall R.A. on Venereal Disease.	
	Apr 12		Training according to programme. Bath for B Coy; A Coy, Cooks & Transport.	
	Apr 13		Church Parade. Presbyterian 0915; C. of E. 1115 R.C. 1015	
	Apr 14		Training as per programme. Officers v Hockey match	
	Apr 15		Training as per programme	
	Apr 16		Training as per programme	

D. D. & L., London, E.C.
(10340) Wt W5500/P713 750,000 3/18 E 2658 Forms/C2118/16

Army Form C. 2118.

WAR DIARY
or
INTELLIGENCE SUMMARY.

(Erase heading not required.)

Place	Date	Hour	Summary of Events and Information	Remarks and references to Appendices
SOLINGEN	4/17		Training as per programme. Battalion & Coy Recreation Committees formed. Coy training Good Friday — observed as a Holiday. Church parades. Gentlemen (voluntary)	
	4/18		at 1015 C. of E. at 1115. R.C. (voluntary) at 1500 Baths for A, B v H Q Coys	
	4/19.	0900 1400 1815	Training as per programme. Baths for C, D Coys. Kit inspection. Company training Competition for Battalion Cup. Cup won by "C" Coy Grand morning Competition, for which turned out on exceptionally fine parade	
	4/20.	0915	Church Parade. Distribution. C. of E. 1115. R.C. 1015.	
	4/21.	900	Training as per programme.	
	4/22.	900	Training as per programme. Inspection of transport by C.O.	
	4/23.	900 1400	Training as per programme. Base Ball Match v. 15th H.L.I.	
	4/24.	900. 8.45. 9.10.	Training as per programme. Inspection of Kitchens Dining Latrines by Sanitary Expert. Working Party detailed for Range. (200 mm A & B Coys). Boats for crews of all Coys.	
	4/25.	900. 1400– 15.30. 1500 to 1700	Training as per programme. Boats for C & D Coys. Baths for A Coy.	
	4/26.	9.30 & 1400	Training as per programme.	

WAR DIARY

or

INTELLIGENCE SUMMARY.

(Erase heading not required.)

Instructions regarding War Diaries and Intelligence
Summaries are contained in F. S. Regs., Part II.
and the Staff Manual respectively. Title pages
will be prepared in manuscript.

Place	Date	Hour	Summary of Events and Information	Remarks and references to Appendices
SOLIN GEN	27/4/19	0845	CHURCH PARADES Breakfasts 0845: C & E. 10.45. RC. 1015	
	28/4/19		Training as per Programme. Battalion Hockey match V 51st H.L.I.	
	29/4/19		Training after Programme 17.30 hrs Lecture. Subject "Life & Amusements of The Ancient Romans" given by Rev Canon Maynard.	
	30/4/19		Training as per Programme.	

D. D. & L., London, E.C.
(1050) Wt W3509/F773 750,000 3/18 E 2688 Forms/C2118/16

J. C. Carmichael
Lieut.-Colonel,
Comdg 1/5th K.O.S. Borderers.

20.W.
4 sheets

DUPLICATE

WAR DIARY

1/5th Bn. KINGS OWN SCOTTISH BORDERERS

FROM 1/5/19   TO   31/5/19

VOLUME XLIX.

WAR DIARY

or

INTELLIGENCE SUMMARY.

(Erase heading not required.)

Instructions regarding War Diaries and Intelligence Summaries are contained in F. S. Regs., Part II and the Staff Manual respectively. Title pages will be prepared in manuscript.

Place	Date	Hour	Summary of Events and Information	Remarks and references to Appendices
SOLINGEN	MAY 1	9.00	Training as per programme in Bng Billets	
	2		Training as per programme.	
			Lt. Col. J. W. Arnolde, D.S.O. assumes command of this Battalion this date.	
			Cologne leave to forty given consent in Homeward.	
	3.	9.00	Training according to Programme	
	4.		Church Parades.	
		9.15	Presbyterians	
		11.15	Church of England.	
		10.15	Roman Catholics	
	5.	9.00	Training as per programme	
	6.	9.00	Training as per programme.	
		18.00	Parade of all Sanitary men and Water-men.	
			Inspection in Bng Billets of all Laundry and Officers and Sgts. from N.C.O.	
			all Bays parade in full strength from this date at 14.00 hrs daily for Sport	
		17.30	Lecture in Homeward By J. D. Vincent Translation subject "INDUSTRIAL RECONSTRUCTION".	
	7.	9.00	Training as per programme	
		10.00	Bath for A B C D Coy. Baths for H.Q. Coy 14.00 to 18.00 hrs.	
			Visit of H R H the Duke of Connaught.	
	8.	9.00	Training as per programme.	
		17.30	Lecture in Homeward by Mr SAMSON PERKINS, subject "MIDST ARCTIC SNOWS"	
	9.	9.00	Training as per programme.	

D. D. & L., London, E.C.
(29301) W. W8900 P713 730,000 3/15 E 2068 Forms/C2118/26

WAR DIARY
or
INTELLIGENCE SUMMARY.

(Erase heading not required.)

Instructions regarding War Diaries and Intelligence Summaries are contained in F. S. Regs., Part II. and the Staff Manual respectively. Title pages will be prepared in manuscript.

Place	Date	Hour	Summary of Events and Information	Remarks and references to Appendices
SOLINGEN	MAY 10	9.m	Training as for programme.	
		10.00	Inspection of Billets, Work-horses etc by Commanding Officer	
			Lts. I.B., Turk takes over Command and duty of D. Cony from the other.	
	11	10.15	Church Parades Presbyterian	
		11.15	Church of England	
		10.15	Roman Catholic	
	12	9.00	Training as for programme.	
	13	9.00	Training as for programme.	
		17.30	Lecture in Hamburg by VEN. ARCHDEACON JINES, Subject BRITISH CHARACTER BUILDERS	
	14	9.m	Training as for programme	
		9.00/2		
		10.00	Bath for A.B.C.D.Coy. Bauport - H.Q. Coy Bath 14.00 to 16.00 hrs.	
	15	9.m	Training as for programme	
		17.30	Lecture in HAIBERSHAL, by MR EDGAR BELLINGHAM. Subject "PEOPLE OF THE DESERT."	
	16	9.00	Training as for programme.	
	17	9.m	Lecture in KAISERSHAL by LT. COL. LYNHAM. Subject "THE FALLACIES OF BOLSHEVISM."	
		10.m	Bath for A and D Coy	
	18		Church Parades	
		9.15	Presbyterian	
		11.15	Church of England	
		10.15	Roman Catholic	
		14.30	Hockey Match 1/6 K.A.S.B. V 5/2TH L.I.	

D. D. & L., London, E.C.
(1450) W.W.3500/P715 750,000 2/16 E.1088 Forms/C2118/16

Army Form C. 2118.

WAR DIARY

or

INTELLIGENCE SUMMARY.

(Erase heading not required.)

Instructions regarding War Diaries and Intelligence
Summaries are contained in F.S. Regs., Part II.
and the Staff Manual respectively. Title pages
will be prepared in manuscript.

Place	Date	Hour	Summary of Events and Information	Remarks and references to Appendices
SOLINGEN	MAY 19	9.00	Training as for programme	
		10.30	Commanding Officers inspection of all billets	
		11.00	Inspection of Medical Officer	
	20	9.00	Training as for programme	
	21	9.00	Training as for programme	
		10.30	Bath for A and B Coys	
	22	9.00	Training according to programme	
		14.00		Regimental street project discontinued
		15.00	Bath for C.D & H.Q. Coys	
	23	9.00	Training as for programme	
	24	9.00	Training as for programme	
		10.30	Commanding Officers inspected H.billets	
		11.00		
		12.00	Bath for Transport and all ranks	
			Church Parade	
	25	9.5	Pay to Coys	
		10.15	Church of England	
		16.15	Roman Catholic	
	26	9.00	Training as for programme	
		14.30	Lecture in KAISERSAAL by REV. T.M. DOUGLAS Subject CONSTANTINOPLE, HISTORY, MONUMENTS and PEOPLE.	
	27	9.40	Battalion Parade. Dress Fighting order	
	28	9.00	Training as for programme	
		9.00	Bath for A and B Coys	
		10.30		
	29	9.00	Battalion Sports 7.K Infantry Brigade	
			Bath for C and H.Q. Coys	
	30	9.00		
		9.30	Training as for programme	
	31	9.00		
			Training as for programme	
		10.00	Bath for Transport	

C. Crum
Lieut.-Colonel.
Comdg. 1/5th K.O.S. Borderers.

15th Kow Bde.
Low Div.

CONFIDENTIAL

WAR DIARY

of

15th Bn KING'S OWN SCOTTISH BORDERERS

FROM 1/6/19   TO 30/6/19

VOLUME I

Army Form C. 2118.

WAR DIARY

or

INTELLIGENCE SUMMARY.

(Erase heading not required.)

Instructions regarding War Diaries and Intelligence Summaries are contained in F. S. Regs., Part II. and the Staff Manual respectively. Title pages will be prepared in manuscript.

Place	Date	Hour	Summary of Events and Information	Remarks and references to Appendices
SOLINGEN				

D. D. & L., London, E. C.
(1899) W¹ W³500/P973 250,000 5/15 E 5558 Forms/C2118/10

WAR DIARY
or
INTELLIGENCE SUMMARY.
(Erase heading not required.)

Instructions regarding War Diaries and Intelligence Summaries are contained in F. S. Regs., Part II. and the Staff Manual respectively. Title pages will be prepared in manuscript.

Place	Date	Hour	Summary of Events and Information	Remarks and references to Appendices
SOLINGEN	June 10	0915	Turnout as per programme	
			Rhine Troop" for 35 mins an detached — Bn Orders	
	11	0900	Company Parade & Inspection Battn 1st "A" "B" Coys	
		0940	Batt Parade	
		1130	Lenten Lecture — Never Sand — by Mr Dqrlough Trees or Eighth it	
	12		Race Sports to Bde "	@45
			Training as per programme	
		0930	Educational Examination (2nd Class Army Certificate Examination) "A" & "B" Coys	
	13	0900	Training & per programme	
		0930	Educational Exam for "C" "D" Coys	
	14	0900	Training as per programme	
	15		Church Parades	
		0915	Picquet, C.E.	
		1015	C.J.E.	
		1015	R.C.	
	16	0915	Battalion Route March	
		0930	Training as per programme	
	17	0900	Batt received Rhine Coy's for men detailed to KETZBERG in position for advance to Elberfeld should there	Bn not be required
	18	0900	Batt received & supplying Bde O.H. Transport & march to KETZBERG arrive about 1100 hrs. From Bde Batt at KETZBERG; H.Q. established in Cafe ZEPPELIN STRASSE Supplies stored to awaiting SOLINGEN. 1/2 of R.O.H.S. Truck & Guard	

Army Form C. 2118.

WAR DIARY

or

INTELLIGENCE SUMMARY.

(*Erase heading not required.*)

Instructions regarding War Diaries and Intelligence
Summaries are contained in F. S. Regs., Part II.
and the Staff Manual respectively. Title pages
will be prepared in manuscript.

Place	Date	Hour	Summary of Events and Information	Remarks and references to Appendices
KETZBERG	19	0900	Battery parade and inspection	
		0930	Battery parade	
	20	0900	Training — Competition programme	
	21	0900	Company parade — attack	
		0230	Inter-Company football — 1 Coy v C.O.	
	22	0900	Major Gen. Tudor G.O.C. L.H.S. Division visited Battalion	
			Presentation of Russian distinction ribbons by R — J.K.3	
	23	0900	Slidge D.D. of M.N.U.S. Unit —	
			C.T.E. R.C. —	
		0930	Conduct Parade —	
			Ambulance placed by O.H.M.S.	
	24	—	Training according to programme	
	25	—	Coy Parades and —	
	26	—	Coy Parades and training	
			Div. Sports and training as per Programme	
	27	2.30	Y inspection Parade by G.O.C	
			Funeral at —	
	28	9.30	Church service — PEACE signed at VERSAILLES	
		9.30	Divine Service —	
	29	—	Church Parade — signed by G.O.	
		—	Training as per programme — at Guard engagement 10.39 disengaged	
	30	—		

.... Lieut.-Colonel.

Comdg 1/5th K.O.S. BORDERERS.

(B20) W.W.g000/P73 750,000 9/18 E 2808 Forms C2118/16   D. D. & L., London, E.C.

5th. Battn. The King's Own Scottish Borderers.

ADVANCE INTO GERMANY.   Copy................ 15.

                5th. K.O.S.B. No. 2.   Ref. Map.
                                                        2 S. N.W.
                                                        1/25,000.

1.   The LOWLAND BRIGADE GROUP will advance on J Day and occupy
        ELBERFELD and high Gound on General Line A.9595-A.8690-A.7680-
        A.6080-A.5680-A.4575-A.3773.

2.   The 15th. H.L.I. "A" Coy. 8th. Cyclists Battalion, "A" Battery
        50th. Brigade R.F.A. will compose the Advance Guard.

3.   The Advance Guard (See Para. 2.) will march by KLUSE-VOHWINKEL-
        WIEDEN-SAARENHAUS-BERGENHEIDE-STEINBERG-BIRKEN-METZ MACHERATH-
        LENGENFELF RD. and will occupy HIGH GROUND as mentioned in Para.
        1.

4.   The Order of march is as follows for the Brigade Group:-

                        {   Brigade Headquarters.
                        {   1st. Lowland T.M.B.
                        {   1.Section 64th. Field Coy. R.E.
        MAIN BODY.   {   1.Coy. 9th. Battn. M.G.C.
                        {   51st. H.L.I.
                        {   5th. Battn. The King's Own Scottish Borderers.
                        {   28th. Field Ambulance.
                        {   105th. Coy. R.A.S.C.

5.   The STARTING point of the main body will be the ROAD JUNCTION
        150 YARDS SOUTH of KLUSE POSE. A. 5612.   The HOUR of passing
        this POINT will be notified later.

6.   The Order of march for the Battalion will be as follows:-

                        Signallers Section and Runners.
                        Band.
                        "B" Coy.
                        "C" Coy.
                        Colour Party.
                        "D" Coy.
                        "A" Coy.
                        Hd. Qrs. Coy.
                        Transport.

7.   ROUTE.

        GRAFRATH-VOHWINKEL-SONNBORN-ELBERFELD ROAD.

8.   The following distances must be strictly maintained.

                20 Yards between Battalions.
                10 Yards between Companies.
                20 Yards between Battalions and other Units.
        Halts will be at 10 Minutes to each Clock Hour during the
        March and will resume at the clock hour.
        Attention is called to pamphlets already issued re March
        discipline.

9.   During the Advance RED Very Lights (1 inch) will be used to
        indicate that the advance is being resisted by the enemy.

10.   On completion of the march the Battalion will be billeted in
        ELBERFELD, Billeting Area will be allotted later.

11. On arrival at ELBERFELD Guards (which will be detailed later) will mount on important Railway Bridges and Tunnels in an AREA allotted to the Battalion i.e., Squares 86, 76, 65, 75, 64, 74. (except Bridges at A. 7864 and A. 7965 and Railways between these Bridges.)

12. On arrival at ELBERFELD 1 Company will be detailed as WALKING PICQUET.

13. A BATTALION ALARM POST will be notified all Companies on arrival.

14. All watches will be SYCHRONISED at BATTN. HD'. QRS. on the Morning of J DAY.

15. J DAY and ZERO HOUR will be notified later.

16. BATTALION HD. QRS. will close at KETZBERG on J DAY at ZERO HOUR minus 60 MINUTES.

17. ACKNOWLEDGE.

[signature]

Capt. and Adjt.

5th. Battn. The King's Own Scottish Borderers.

20/6/1919.

DISTRIBUTION.

Copy No.	1.	Commanding Officer.
" "	2.	2nd. in Command.
" "	3.	Adjutant.
" "	4.	Q.M.
" "	5.	T.O.
" "	6.	M.O.
" "	7.	Signal Officer.
" "	8.	O. C. "A" Coy.
" "	9.	O. C. "B" Coy.
" "	10.	O. C. "C" Coy.
" "	11.	O. C. "D" Coy.
" "	12.	O. C. Hd. Qrs. Coy.
" "	13.	R.S.M.
" "	14.	File.
" "	15.	War Diary.
" "	16.	" "
" "	17.	Spare Copy.

Copy........ 16

SECRET.   O P E R A T I O N   O R D E R   No. 1.
-------   by
            Lieut. Col. J.C.W. Connell. D.S.O.   Map Ref. Germany, 2".
   Commanding 5th. Battn. The King's Own Scottish Borderers, 17/6/19.
==
               Ref. Special Order No. 1. and Coy. Commanders
                          Conference to-day.
               ----

1. The Battalion(less special Rear Party detailed) will parade in
   fighting order at Battn. Hd. Qrs. at 0900 hours, 18th. inst. The
   Transport WILL BE DRAWN up facing S.E. along SCHWERTZ STRASSE by
2. 0915 hours.

2. The Battalion will move forward to KETZBERG(3 miles.) to billets
   already fixed. Billeting party will meet Companies on arrival.

3. An Advanced Guard of two platoons will be furnished by O.C. "A" Coy.

4. Order of March.

               Band.
               Hd. Qrs. Signallers and Runners.
               "A" Coy.
               "B" Coy.
               "C" Coy.
               "D" Coy.
               Hd. Qrs. Coy.
               Transport.

5. L.G. Limbers and Pack Animals will march with their Companies, Cookers
   will march in rear with Battalion Transport.

6. Horses for L.G. Limbers will report to Company Hd. Qrs. early on
   morning of 18th. inst.

7. Pack Animals will report at Battn. Hd. Qrs. at 0800 hours, 18th. inst.
   for loading, and will join their Companies at Battn. Parade ground.

8. Motor Lorries will report at 0730 hours on the morning of the 18th.
   inst to pick up from Coy. Hd. Qrs. Blankets, Officers Kits, Orderly
   Room Kit. Guides will be found by Q.M.

9. The following rear party will left in charge of Battn. Hd. Qrs. and
   Stores.

       240105. R.Q.M.S. Sinclair G.W. }
       43574   Pte.   Thomson N.   } Q.M. Stores.

       Guard.
       240179. Sgt.   Ferguson T.   Orderly Room.
       343937 Pte.   Spivey H.
       45116.   "   Love A.
       41654   "   Farquharson J.
       34179   "   McKinna. W.
       44737   L/Cpl.   Wilson W.
       43027   Pte.   McKenzie J.
       34322   "   Colquhoun.

   These will rationed up to and including 22nd. inst.

10. Balmorals hats will be carried underneath straps of the haversack.

11. O.C. "E" Coy. will furnish the Hd. Qrs. Guard and Officers Mess Guard
    on the arrival at new billets. These will be same numbers as usual.

12. Reveille will be 0500 hours. Breakfasts 0630 hours.

13. O.C. Coys will report to Orderly Room directly all their men are settl
    in new Billets.

APPENDIX TO WAR DIARY.

	Officers	O.R's.
Strength at 31st of last month	49	557.
Sick invalided and Transferred during month	1	21.
Reinforcements during month		2.
Demobilised during month		5.
Strength as at 30th of present month	52	550.

Lieut.Colonel.

3.6.19.   Commanding 5th Batt.The King's Own Scottish Borderers.

CONFIDENTIAL

WAR DIARY

of

1/5th Bn. KING'S OWN SCOTTISH BORDERERS

FROM 1/4/19.

To. 03/7/19.

VOLUME LI.

WAR DIARY.

OF

THE 5TH BATTN. THE KINGS OWN SCOTTISH BORDERERS.

JULY 1919.

WAR DIARY

or

INTELLIGENCE SUMMARY.

(Erase heading not required.)

Instructions regarding War Diaries and Intelligence
Summaries are contained in F. S. Regs., Part II.
and the Staff Manual respectively. Title pages
will be prepared in manuscript.

Place	Date	Hour	Summary of Events and Information	Remarks and references to Appendices
KETSBERG	JULY 1	9.30	Bus. Parade on Fortress Ground. Reading Sunday service out as per Programme	
"	2	8.30	Move Pioneer dept to estany L.O., Read & 43 oct.	
"		1.50	Divisional Parade. Drill order.	
COLINGEN	3	9.30	Division move to the SOLINGEN AREA as per OPERATION ORDER No 2 f the 28/6/14. Training as per programme.	
"	4		That day turned out a General Holiday by the troops f I II Corps. Sports Comp. held on ground. RITTER STRASS B. and HEATS run off. f Sports XMTT. SPORTS.	
"	5	8.30	Dept formed on BARTHS GROUND. SCANERT STRASSE.	
"		10.00	S.O.S. inspection f others	
"	6		Church Parade	
"		9.15	Helgeland and Stand f England. Hours thanksgiving service.	
"		7.45	Roman Parade	
"	7	9.30	Training according to programme	
"	8	9.30	Evening [?] per programme. Major g R.O. TRAPPES D.S.O. M.C. attend. Dismissed f the troops during the week. T Raid S/E g J.S.4 & brevice O.S.O. and are to E.K.	
"	9	9.30	Training as per Programme	
"		10.30	Dept for aid Manual	
"	10	9.30	All troops sent out thoroughly clean and tidy.	
"	11		Division visited the 20th K.R.R.C. 93rd Division at ZONS — STURTEL BURG were turned out for the INSTRUCTIONS No I..." ...	
ZONS	12	9.15	G.S. Inspection g the Place. Billettigen and Organising Service, who supply in and turned out Billetts	

D. D. & L., London, E.C.
(10540) W† W†300/PP15 730,000 3/16 E 5858 Forms/C2118/16

WAR DIARY

or

INTELLIGENCE SUMMARY.

(*Erase heading not required.*)

Instructions regarding War Diaries and Intelligence Summaries are contained in F. S. Regs., Part II. and the Staff Manual respectively. Title pages will be prepared in manuscript.

Place	Date	Hour	Summary of Events and Information	Remarks and references to Appendices
ZON S	July 13	9.00	Inspection at the Regimental School	
		11.00	Subjobian Church Parades & B. 7. 5.	
		9.00	Review Scheme do.	
		14	9.00	Training as per Programme issued	
		15	9.00	Brendon Parade	
			9.30	Training according to Plan	
		16	9.00	Battalion Parade	
			9.30	Training as per Programme above	
		17	9.00	Training as per Programme issued	
				Parade to Church Parade	
			9.30–D³	8.60–A Coy 9.30–G Coy 10.30–8 Coy	
			11.00	Inspection by Brigadier the O.C. the Regiment	Lt. Col. Young C.O. appointed
		18	9.30	Training as per Programme issued	
			11.30	Inspection by Brigade Gen. D.C.O. of E.	Capt. Young C.O. Adjutant
		19	—	HOLIDAY. BATTALION SPORTS MEETING	
		20	—	Church Parade	
			10.00	Thanksgiving Service of Progress	
			9.31	Kirken Evening	
		21	9.00	Training as per Programme	
		22	9.00	Training as per Programme issued	
		23	9.00	Training as per Programme	
				Lecture to the Officers' Mess Dist. by Major Wade on post War Savings Certificates	

D. D. & L., London, L.C.

(8930) Wt W3900/P743 750,000 3/15 E 2858 Forms/Can5/16

Army Form C. 2118.

WAR DIARY
— or —
INTELLIGENCE SUMMARY.

(Erase heading not required.)

Instructions regarding War Diaries and Intelligence Summaries are contained in F. S. Regs., Part II and the Staff Manual respectively. Title pages will be prepared in manuscript.

Place	Date	Hour	Summary of Events and Information	Remarks and references to Appendices
ZONS	July 24	7.00	Training according to Programme issued.	
		7.30	B Coy. 8.30 A Coy. 9.30 C Coy. 10.30 B Coy.	
	25th	9.30	Training as per programme.	
	26th	10.00	Commanding Officers Inspection of troops.	
		11.30	Education Training.	
	27th		Divine Service.	
		9.30	Church Parade.	
		2.30	Recreational Games & Sports of England.	
	28	9.00	Training as per programme issued.	
	29	9.00	Training as per programme.	
			Lt. Col. J.C.W. Connell returned from U.K. leave 23/7/19 and taken up again command over command of the Battalion and dis	
	30	9.00	Training as per programme issued.	
	31	9.00	Training as per Programme issued.	

C. Connell
Lt. Col.
Comg. 1/5th R.G.S.

D. D. & L., London, E.C.

WAR DIARY
or
INTELLIGENCE SUMMARY.

(Erase heading not required.)

Army Form C. 2118.

Instructions regarding War Diaries and Intelligence Summaries are contained in F. S. Regs., Part II. and the Staff Manual respectively. Title pages will be prepared in manuscript.

Place.	Date	Hour	Summary of Events and Information	Remarks and references to Appendices
Grafrath Army July	1st		Showery. Batt. prepare to move back to their original Billets in Istrugen.	TM
Istrugen Army	2nd		Very showery. Batt. move back to Istrugen.	TM
	3+4		Dull and showery. Training under Coy. arrangements	TM
	4th		Mild. Holiday.	TM
	5th		Very warm. Lt Col. Y.L. Thackeray D.S.O. joins Batt. and assumes command from this date. Major AB Thurburn takes over duties of Second in Command.	RP
	6th		Dull-mild. Church Parade as usual. — Special Orders Thanksgiving Service. Major-General Byrne DSO. inb. proceeds to 51st D.L.9.	TM
	½		Dull. Section training under Coy. arrangements. Battalion photographed by Official Photographer. Musketry Match v 51st Manch. Result 15th D.L.9. = 39. 51st Manch: 30.	TM
	8th		Dull. Section training under Coy. arrangements. 'C' Coy. on Bukeberg Range.	TM
	9th		Dull. Showery. Section training under Coy. arrangements. 'C' Coy on Bukeberg Range.	TM
	10th		Showery. Battalion preparing to move. Inland Rwagon being relieved by Rugbi. Brown, 13th & L.9. being relieved by 13th K.R.R.C. Advance party of K.R.R.C. took over Othes Railhead Guard.	TM
	11th		Heavy rain. Battalion move to Dummagen.	TM

(49475) Wt W3355/P350 600,000 12/7 D. D.&L. Sch.52a Forms/C2118/13

Army Form C. 2118.

WAR DIARY
or
INTELLIGENCE SUMMARY

(Erase heading not required.)

Instructions regarding War Diaries and Intelligence
Summaries are contained in F. S. Regs., Part II.
and the Staff Manual respectively. Title Pages
will be prepared in manuscript.

Place	Date	Hour	Summary of Events and Information	Remarks and references to Appendices
Remagen. Germany	July 12th		Showery. Cleaning rifles. Rifles inspection by C.O. Lt.Col. J.J. Hackeray proceeds to join 2nd Bn. Lt.Col. A.B. Tarbeton to assume command.	TBP
	13th		Showery. Church Parade in Swimming Baths.	TBP
	14th		Dull, mild. Training under Coy. arrangement. 2Lt. D. 1P. MacIntyre returned from leave.	TBP
	15th		Mild. Training under Coy. arrangement. Inter Coy. Cricket match. "A" Coy. v. H.Qrs. Coy. Win for H.Qrs. Coy.	TBP
	16th		Warm. Training under Coy. arrangement. Cricket match 51st M.R. 9. x 15th A.R. 9. Won by about 40 runs.	TBP
	17th		Very warm. Training under Coy. arrangements.	TBP
	18th		Mild. Training under Coy. arrangements.	TBP
	19th		Very warm. Heavy thunderstorm in afternoon. Whole holiday. 6-a-side sports in afternoon.	TBP
			Showery. Church Parade as usual. Cricket match. Officers v. N.C.O's & men. Win No. O's & men 86. Officers 31.	TBP
	20th		Very wet. "A" & "B" Coy. on Company training. "C" "D" Coy. training under Coy. arrangements. "A" Coy. transport field sport in afternoon.	TBP
	21st		Wet. "A" & "B" Coy. on Coy. training. "B" "D" Coy. under Coy. arrangement.	TBP
	22nd		Brigade Lacrosse at Chequal of H.Coy. "D" Coy. under Coy. arrangement.	TBP
	23rd		Showery. "A" & "B" Coy. on Coy. training. "C" "D" under Coy. arrangement. Lecture by Major Waite on War Savings & Afterwards. Orders Coy. Orrols County H.Q. B.10. bomb: 3M. H.G. 210. bomb: 2M D 119 bomb. 222 D 83 bomb. 222 D 83 bomb. 4M B. 1001. 310.	TBP

Army Form C. 2118.

WAR DIARY
or
INTELLIGENCE SUMMARY
(Erase heading not required.)

Instructions regarding War Diaries and Intelligence
Summaries are contained in F. S. Regs., Part II.
and the Staff Manual respectively. Title Pages
will be prepared in manuscript.

Place	Date	Hour	Summary of Events and Information	Remarks and references to Appendices
Germany Germany	July 23rd (cont.)	5.15 p.m.	Bomb. Individual winner - 13th Pte. Drysdale. "A" Coy. 2nd Pte. Pain.	7/P
			385 points.	7/P
	24th	2 p.m.	Duration. "A" Coy. 3rd 2/Lt. McDonald. "D" Coy. 4th Pte. Barclay. "D" Coy.	7/P
	25th	9 a.m.	B. Coy. on Company training.	7/P
			"A" + "B" Coy. on bombing training. C + D under Coy. arrangements.	7/P
	26th		Preliminary Rise of Battalion Sports were off. Boot came on dismissal.	7/P
			Duff. - Wet. Battalion Sports held. Lunch band in attendance. Prizes presented by	7/P
			Brig. Gen. Carlos Cambrell. Coy. championship won by Coy. Runners up :- Coy.	
			Individual winner - Pte. Drysdale. "A" Coy. Runner up :- Pte. Daniels.	7/P
	27th	9 a.m.	Duff. - Wet. Church Parade cancelled in afternoon - 15th K.R.S. + 2/G.S.	
			15th dis. Handsome win for 15th K.R.S. Capt. McFarLane joined Battalion and	7/P
			assumed duty as Signal in command.	
	28th		Duff. A + B. Coy. on Company training.	7/P
	29th	9 a.m.	Very Wet. Training as yesterday.	7/P
	30th	9 a.m.	Duff. Training as for previous day. Football match. 15th K.R.S. + 15th K.O.S.B. Win for	7/P
			K.R.S. 9 - 1 Goals to 3.	
	31st		Duff. Training as for previous day. Church on for previous day. Bom. Ltt. Hecker 1 Sar.	7/P
			Bn. Bomb. as dispersal. C.O.'s Coy. Party left for Germans billeting stations.	

	Offrs.	N.C.O.s	Men	
Commanding Officer's Strength.		34	415	1007
Fighting Strength.		32	411	462
		26	24	462
		1	311	492

2449 Wt. W14957/M90 750,000 1/16 J.B.C. & A. Form/C.2118/12.

(signature) Commanding 15th K.R.S.

War Diary -

51st Bn. Highland Light Infantry

July 1919

D. R. Murray Lyon

Major

Commanding 51st Bn. High. L. Infy.

WAR DIARY

or

~~INTELLIGENCE SUMMARY~~

(Erase heading not required.)

Instructions regarding War Diaries and Intelligence Summaries are contained in F. S. Regs., Part II. and the Staff Manual respectively. Title Pages will be prepared in manuscript.

Place	Date	Hour	Summary of Events and Information	Remarks and references to Appendices
Solingen	1/7/19		Training as per programme	
	2/7/19		Take over Cricket bus from 5i at Gordon Highlanders	
	3/7/19		Training as per programme.	
	4/7/19.		Observed as a holiday	
	5/7/19.		Training as per programme	
	6/7/19.		Church Parade	
	7/7/19.		Training as for programme	
	8/7/19		Do.	
	9/7/19.		Do.	
	10/7/19		Bath. for C Company.	
Sonningen	11/7/19.		Training as per programme	
	12/7/19		Battalion move from Solingen area to Sonningen area.	
	13/7/19		Training as per programme	
	14/7/19		Church Parade	
	15/7/19		Training as per programme.	
	16/7/19		Do	
	17/7/19.		Do	

2449 Wt. W14957/M90 750,000 1/16 J.B.C. & A. Forms/C.2118/12.

Army Form C. 2118.

WAR DIARY
or
INTELLIGENCE SUMMARY

(Erase heading not required.)

Instructions regarding War Diaries and Intelligence Summaries are contained in F. S. Regs., Part II. and the Staff Manual respectively. Title Pages will be prepared in manuscript.

Place	Date	Hour	Summary of Events and Information	Remarks and references to Appendices
Warrington	18/7/19		Training as per programme	
	19/7/19		Baths for C.L. & A.2 Cos. Examination on the Standard of Army Certificate "B" Coy.	
	20/7/19		Training as per programme. Baths for "B" Co. Training as per programme.	
	21/7/19		Examination on the Standard of Army Certificate "A" Coy	
	22/7/19		Training as per programme Examination on the Standard of Army Certificate "C" Coy.	
	23/7/19		Training as per programme	
	24/7/19		Lecture by Major Wade on "War Aims". Exam 9' Certificate	
	25/7/19		Examination on the Standard of Army Certificate "D" Coy	
	26/7/19		Training as per programme	
	27/7/19		Do. Church Parade.	
	28/7/19		Battalion Sports Meeting	
	29/7/19		Training as per programme	
	30/7/19		Baths for "A" & "D" Coy. "D" Coy	
	31/7/19		Training as per programme	

2449 Wt. W4957/M90 750,000 1/16 J.B.C. & A. Forms/C.2118/12.

Army Form C. 2118.

WAR DIARY

OR

INTELLIGENCE SUMMARY.

(Erase heading not required.)

Instructions regarding War Diaries and Intelligence Summaries are contained in F. S. Regs., Part II. and the Staff Manual respectively. Title pages will be prepared in manuscript.

Place	Date	Hour	Summary of Events and Information	Remarks and references to Appendices
KETSBERG	JULY 1	7.30	Bttn. Parade on Football Ground. Revelry. Training carried out as for Programme.	
	" 2	9.30	Fixie Overseas trips to totary. 2 Off & 40 O.Rs. Operation Parade. Sport Order.	
	" 3	1.50	Battalion move to the SOLINGEN AREA as for OPERATION ORDER No 3, 9th June 29/6/19	
	" 4	9.30	Training as per Programme.	
SOLINGEN	" 5		This day ground is a General Holiday as we Crafts of IX Corps Hold meeting held on ground KITTEL STRASSE and NEATS run off Sports BATT. SPORTS	
	" 6	9.30 9.00	Bttn. Parade on Battn GROUND, SCHNUERT STRASSE. C.O. inspection or Inspect.	
	"		Church Parades	
	"	9.15 7.15	Regimental and Church of England. Roman Catholic. Church Thanksgiving Service.	
	" 7	10.00	Training according to Programme issued.	
	" 8	9.30	Training as per Programme.	
	"		Major G.A.S. Thomas D.S.O. who resumed command of the Bttn during the rence of Lut. Col. Y.... you relaxed D.S.O. on leave to U.K.	
	"	4.30 10.30	Training as for Programme. Church for as Usual.	
	" 9	9.30	The Brigade Bomb and Lewis.gy class ran rule. Bombers under the S.I.S. K.R.R.C. Lewis Division at ZONS - STURZELBURG Lewis matter now as for INSTRUCTIONS NO 1. space.	
ZONS	" 10	9.15	Whitsun. Bttn. move away in the Evening Buses, Lorrups, as were issued out Busts	

D. D. & L., London, E.C.
(1030) Wt W3500/P715 750,000 5/18 E 2858 Forms/C2118/16

Army Form C. 2118.

WAR DIARY

or

INTELLIGENCE SUMMARY.

(*Erase heading not required.*)

Instructions regarding War Diaries and Intelligence Summaries are contained in F. S. Regs., Part II. and the Staff Manual respectively. Title pages will be prepared in manuscript.

Place	Date	Hour	Summary of Events and Information	Remarks and references to Appendices
ZON?	July?	9.30		
		11.30		

B. D. & L., London, E.C.
(1413) W18 W3500/P713 750,000 3/15 E 2688 Forms,C2118/16

WAR DIARY
or
INTELLIGENCE SUMMARY.
(Erase heading not required.)

Instructions regarding War Diaries and Intelligence Summaries are contained in F. S. Regs., Part II. and the Staff Manual respectively. Title pages will be prepared in manuscript.

Place	Date	Hour	Summary of Events and Information	Remarks and references to Appendices
ZONS	July 11	9.00	Training according to Programme attached	
			Detail:-	
		D.60?		
		7.30	R.S.S A.C? 7.30 C.C? 10.30 D.60?	
	28?	9.00	Training as per programme	
		10.700?	Commanding Officers Inspection of Drills	
		1.30	Educational Training	
			Games, Sports	
		8.10	Reveille Parade	
		1.00	integration & guard of England	
	29	9.00	Training as per programme	
			carried as per programme	
			4 men from Event returns from M.B came 2/11/18 all soldiers again	
			took over command of the Battalion as a whole	
	30	9.00	Training as per movement area	
	31	4.00	Training as per programme detail	

D. D. & L., London, E.C.
(6090) W. W.3900/1773 750,000 5/15 E 8658 Forms/C.2118/10

MOVE TO ZONS-STURZELBURG AREA.

5th. K.O.S.B. Instructions No. 1.

9th. July 1919.
Ref. Map. 1.K. 1/100000.
2.K. 1/100000.

1. The Battalion will relieve the 20th. K.R.R.C. at ZONS-STURZELBURG on Friday, 11/7/19.   Dress:- Full Marching Order.

2. **Advance Parties.**

Advance Parties as under will move to New Area on 10th. inst. for purpose of taking over and guiding Companies to their Billeting Area.

Officers Mess at 0800.	Orderly Room at 0845.
Capt. Wynne.	C.Q.M.S. "C" Coy.
2nd. Lieut. Wallbank.	" "D" Coy.
Pte. Love.	Sgt. Hd. Qrs. Coy.
C.Q.M.S. "A" Coy.	Pte. Bothwell.
" "B" Coy.	Pte. Matthews.
1. O/R. Q.M. Stores.	1. O/R. Transport.
	Pte. Macfarlane.

The Orderly Officer will march party which is to parade at Orderly Room and report to Bde. Hd. Qrs. by 0930 hours. The unconsumed portion of days rations and rations for 11th. inst. will be taken.   Kits will be taken, also Blankets.

3. **Routine.**

Reveille will be at 0430 hours.
Breakfast...........0530 hours.
The unexpired portion of days rations will be carried by each man.   Tea will be served as soon as possible on arrival at new area.

4. **Guards**

"A" Coy. will furnish a Guard of 1 section not less than 1 N.C.O. and 6 men, relieving Gaurd of 20th. K.R.R.C. at ST PETERS CROSS ROADS POST. They will proceed by the 13.12 train from SOLINGEN to-morrow the 10th. inst.   Rations for 10th. and 11th. inst will be taken, also 1 blanket per man.

5. **Billets.**

O.C. Coys. will certify that all Billets have been left scrupuously clean and will report to Orderly Room when men are settled in new Billets.

6. **Entraining.**

O.C. Coys. will march independently to Station and rendezvous in Yard adjoining Station by 0720 hours.
1 Marker will report to R.S.M. at the Station by 0715 hours.
Each Company will detail a Company Orderly Officer who will report to Adjutant by 0730 and will be given Train allotment. He will also be responsible for train discipline of Company for journey.
Coys. will march on platform and halt facing Train in fours.
No man must be allowed to entrain until an order is / given /

by an Officer. 1 N.C.O. will be detailed to take charge of each
compartment. Regimental Police will be responsible that no men leave
trains until ordered to do so. O.C. "D" will detail 1 N.C.O. and
6 men to load and unload baggage and proceed with baggage train.
They will report to Q.M. at Station by 0645 hours.
Entraining states will be rendered to Orderly Room by O.C.Coys.
by 1000 hours on the 10th inst.
O.C. Transport will send a G.S.Limber to Coy. H.Q. to collect
cooking utensils and report at Station by 0725 hours.
1 cook will proceed with each Coy. cooker, the remainder will
parade with Coys.
1 L.G. to be detailed to proceed with each L.G.Limber.

7. Stores.

All Coy. stores will be stacked at Coy. H.Q. by 1730 hours 10th
inst. and will be collected by lorries. All blankets and Kit.Bags
and Officers Kits must be stacked by 0630 hours on morning of 11th
at Coy. H.Q. and Officers Mess respectively. Coy. storeman will be
responsible for all Coy. stores and will proceed with lorries. All
second suits will be gathered under Coy. arrangements and sent as
Coy. stores. No man is allowed to carry in boxes any surplus kit.

8. Bathing.

No bathing in the New Area is allowed until instructions are
issued. O.C. Coys. must see that this order is rigidly enforced

9. Transport.

Head of Column must be at Cross Roads LILLINGHOFFEN F 4563 on the
SOLINGEN - OHLIGS Road by 0900 hours on the 11th inst. They will
water and feed at BENRATH before embarking. After crossing
they will move independently to join B.H.Q. at ZONN.
L.G. Limbers will be loaded by 1700 hours on the 10th inst. and will
afterwards report to Transport Lines where picquet will be
responsible for safety.

10. Detraining.

No man will detrain until order is given. If ground is suitable
Coys. will form up in close column. Coy. Q.M.Sgts. will report to
O.C.Coy. on arrival.

11. Acknowledge.

Distribution.

Copy No. 1.............Commanding Officer. Copy No.9....O.C. "C" Coy.
          2.............2nd. In Command.   10....O.C. "D" Coy.
          3.............Adjutant.   11....O.C.H.Qrs.Coy.
          4.............Q.M.   12....Sig.Officer.
          5.............T.O.   13....War Diary.
          6.............M.O.   14..... do.
          7.............O.C. "A" Coy.   15....R.S.M.
          8.............O.C. "B" Coy.   16....File.
                   17......Spare Copy.

                              T. Shaw.   2nd.Lt.Act/Adjt.
                              5th Batt.The King's Own Scottish Bdrs.

WAR DIARY

of

5th BATT. KINGS OWN SCOTTISH BORDERERS

Aug 1st 1919 to August 31st 1919

WAR DIARY

INTELLIGENCE SUMMARY.

(Erase heading not required.)

Instructions regarding War Diaries and Intelligence
Summaries are contained in F. S. Regs., Part II.
and the Staff Manual respectively. Title pages
will be prepared in manuscript.

Place	Date	Hour	Summary of Events and Information	Remarks and references to Appendices
ZONS	Aug. 1	9.00	Training carried out as per Programme issued	
		9.30	Inspection of Billets by Go Medical Officer	
	2	10.00	Ceremonial Oparade inspection of Billets	
	3	9.30	Programme and Guard of Englad Church Parade	
		4.30	to be attended. Church Parade.	
	4		The Day spent as a training day.	
	5	9.00	Training as per Programme issued	
			Sunday. Decoration for any Companies	
	6	9.00	Training as per Training Programme issued.	
		11.30	Lecture to Concert Hall by Major A.H. MacBonger D.S.O. Subject STRESS OF WAR UPON THE RACE	
	7	9.00	Training as per Programme	
		7.30 to	Bread for all Companies at Fairey Donagan	
		11.30		
	8	9.00	Training as per Programme issued	
		11-11	Bread for the Coy. and Transport.	
		6.30 a.m		
	9	10.00	Commanding Officers Inspection of parade.	
			Church Parade.	
	10	9.00	Arms Parade.	
		9.30	Boot Inspection.	
		11.00	Church Sunday	
	11	9.00	Training as per Programme issued.	

D. D. & L. London, E.C.
(8930) W1 W3300/P73 750,000 7/15 E 2868 Forms/Cards/16

Army Form C. 2118.

WAR DIARY

or

INTELLIGENCE SUMMARY.

(Erase heading not required.)

Instructions regarding War Diaries and Intelligence Summaries are contained in F. S. Regs., Part II. and the Staff Manual respectively. Title pages will be prepared in manuscript.

Place	Date	Hour	Summary of Events and Information	Remarks and references to Appendices
ZONS.	Aug. 12.	9.00.	Training carried out as per Programme issued.	
	" 13.	9.00.	Training as per Programme	
	" 14.	9.00.	Training as per Programme	
		7.30 8 11.30	Draft for 20 Companies at Theory. Storage	
	" 15.	9.00.	Training carried out as per Programme issued.	
		10.30 15.00.	Draft for Headquarters and Transport Section	
	" 16.	9.00.	Training as per Programme	
	" 17.	9.00.	Roman Catholic Church Parade.	
		9.30	Presbyterian Do Do	
		11.00.	Church of England Do Do.	
	" 18.	9.00.	Training as per Programme issued.	
	" 19.	9.00.	Training carried out as per Programme issued	
	" 20.	9.00.	Training carried out as per Programme issued	
	" 21.	9.00.	Training carried out as per Programme issued	
		10.30 11.30	Draft for all Companies	
	" 22.	9.00.	Training as per Programme	
		10.30 15.00.	Draft for Headquarters and Transport Section	
	" 23.	10.00.	Commanding Officers inspection of Draft.	

D. D. & L., London, L.C.
Wt W3500/713 750,000 3/15 E 2658 Forms/C2118/16

Army Form C. 2118.

WAR DIARY
INTELLIGENCE SUMMARY.

(Erase heading not required.)

Instructions regarding War Diaries and Intelligence Summaries are contained in F. S. Regs., Part II. and the Staff Manual respectively. Title pages will be prepared in manuscript.

Place	Date	Hour	Summary of Events and Information	Remarks and references to Appendices
ZOMS.	Aug 24	9.00	Roman Catholic Church Parade	
		9.30	Programme as if E. Do. Do.	
	" 25	9.00	Training as per Programme Parade	
		11.30	LECTURE. By Capt. H.M. Seddy Regr ... Obert Mal... 23ND	
			SUBJECT :— THE HUNTER AND FISHERMAN IN FOREIGN LANDS	
	" 26	9.00	Training carried out as per Programme issued	
	" 27	9.00	Training carried out as per Programme issued	
	" 28	9.00	Training carried out as per Programme issued	
	" 29	9.00	Training as per Programme issued	Lines Fatigue Ex. X
		15.00	Boat for Headquarters and Trensport Somme	
		17.00	Commanding Officers inspection of Billets	
	" 30	9.00	Roman Catholic Church Parade	
		9.30	Church of England Do. Do.	
	" 31	9.31	Inspection Es. Do.	

D. D. & L., London, L.C.
(10500) Wt W3500/P713 750,000 3/25 & 2888 Forms/C2118/16

22nd. August 1919.

War Diary

1. Herewith Copy of General Instructions for Transfer of the
    Battalion to the U.K.

2. The date on which the Battalion will move is not yet known.
    but it will probably be during the 3rd week og September.
    but Coys. must be prepared to move earlier than this.

3. The number of riders to be taken, the dates on which Iron
    Ration, second suit of clean clothing and Field Dressings
    will be drawn will be notified later.

                                              T. Law   2nd. Lieut. A/Adj.

                              5th Batt. The King's Own Scottish Bdrs

Distribution.

Copy. No. 1. Commanding Officer
  "   " 2. 2nd. in Command.
  "   " 3. Adjutant.
  "   " 4. O.C. "A" Coy.
  "   " 5. O.C. "B" Coy.
  "   " 6. O.C. "C" Coy.
  "   " 7. O.C. "D" Coy.
  "   " C. O.C. Headquarters.
  "   " 9. Quarter Master.
  "   " 10. Medical Officer.
  "   " 11. Signal   "
  "   " 12. Transport "
  "   " 13. War Diary. "
  "   " 14. File.
  "   " 15. Spare Copy.
  "   " 16. R.S.M.

Move Order No. 1.

TRANSFER OF BATTALION TO UNITED KINGDOM.   GENERAL INSTRUCTIONS.

1.   Personnel Trains.

Personnel with arms, equipment, and Lewis Guns complete will
move by rail via Boulogne or Calais. Composition of trains
47 covers,1 coach, 2 brakes. Length of journey by rail about
30 hours. Not more than a proportion of 1 Officer to 30 O.R's
will be despatched to Boulogne as accomodation at this port is
limited.

2.   Equipment Trains.

(1) Vehicles and Regimental equipment will proceed by rail via
    Antwerp and will be loaded at entrainment station by a
    party to be detailed later. Composition of trains 35 flats
    1 coach,3 covers. Length of Journey by rail.—about 14 hours
(2) The baggage and supply waggons shown in war establishment
    as attached to Units will accompany the Transport and will
    not move with Divisional Train.

3.   Motor Transport.

All Motor Transport will proceed to Calais for transhipment
to England by Channel Ferry.

4.   Animals.

Animals will be sent via Calais under seperate instructions
as animals will probably proceed Transport. Transport arrangements will be made to provide necessary animals to move Transport
to entraining station. Each Infantry Brigade will probably
be allotted 24cenders on horse train. Additional horses may
have to be sent for general purposes and instructions to be
issued later.(H.D.will not be included) In such case the con-
ducting parties will be on scale of 1 man for 2 horses.

5.   Advance Party.

Advance Party will be sent entraining by the first personnel
train leaving station.

6.   Entrainment & Detrainment.

A Staff Officer will generally supervise the entrainment &
detrainment at each station. In addition 2nd.Lieut.R.Wallbank
will supervise all entraining and detraining and assist R.T.O.
at each station.

7.   Entraining States.

O.C. All Coys., Quartermaster,and Transport Officer will hand
to Adjt.at a time to be notified later for the following:—
(1) Number of officers and O.R's who will entrain.
(2)   "   of vehicles 4 wheeled and limbered.
(3)   "   of vehicles 4 wheeled and not limbered.
(4)   "   of vehicles 2 wheeled.

Para 7. cont.

(5) Ammount of baggage and tons, stobes etc., other than in vehicles.

All vehicles packages etc., are to be clearly marked with name of Unit. All packages must be securely fastened All concerned should ensure at once that ample boxes and packing necessary are available.

8. Times of reporting to R.T.O.

The Battalion will report to R.T.O. at entraining station as follows:-
for personnel train .....1 hour before scheduled time of departure of trains.
for equipment trains 3 hours.   do.

9. Loading & Unloading Parties.

These will be detailed later (parties at Antwerp will be provided by the Base Commandant).

10. Train Discipline.

(1) Entrainment will be completed 40 minutes before time of departure of train.
(2) No soldier will detrain at any time unless ordered by an Officer.
(3) All doors on the right hand side (left hand side in Germany) will be kept closed,
(4) Brake vans are entirely for use of Railway staff neither personnel nor baggage may be loaded in them.
(5) Carriages and station premises are to be left scrupulously clean.
(6) The R.T.O. is in supreme control at his Station, his decision on all matters relating to railway working is final.

11. Supplies.

(1) All men will entrain with rations sufficient to last them up to and including the day after entrainment
(2) Each Officer and O.R. will carry Iron Rations.

12. Halte Repas.

Halte Repas will be provided at Huy, Charleroi, Ghislingion, and Morris. The times of halting will be notified later. NOTE:- As French money only can be accepted at Halte Repas. O.C. Coys. will ensure that there men are paid out in French Currency prior to entraining.

13. Ordnance.

The clothing as laid down in A.R.O. 2879 will be taken by the man together with the second suit issued under 2nd. Army Routine Order 2433. of 24/1/19.
The question of Transport of 2nd. suit is under consideration at G.H.Q.

Para 13. cont.

In the meantime however Coys. shouls consider the best method to adopt in the case of men without kitbags. It is suggested that bales or packing cases might be used.

(2) Box respirator will be carried on the person.

(3) Stores of value and easily portable.e.g.Bycicles,watches, compasses telescopes,and rifles with teloscopic sights will be handed in to Ordnance under arrangements to be made by D.A.D.O.S. Lists will be obtained in duplicate of all stores so handed in and a receipt obtained on one copy. the other being retained by the Officer to whom the stores are handed over. No equipment in G.1098 which is unserviceable will be taken to U.K. unservice-able articles should only be replaced if required for immediate use. Mere deficiencies in A.F.G. 1098 will not be made good. Certificates from C.O. will be rendered at all surplus stores have been handed in to D.A.D.O.S. with a statement of deficiencies under A.F.G.1098. All stores and equipment surplus to A.F.G.1098 are to be handed into Ordnance under instructions to be issued by D.A.D.O.S. List of articles so handed over are to be rendered to the Ordnance Officer taking them over.

(4) All tentage will be handed in to D.A.D.O.S. as soon as it becomes available but in any case must be handed in prior to departure.

(5) 1 blanket will accompany each man. Other blankets being handed in under sub para 4.

NOTE:- Typewriters and duplicators will accompany Battn. a return will be forwarded to D.D.A.P. & S.S. showing make and registered number of machine.

14. **Baths.**

(1) All men will be bathed and deloused before entraining. if possible.

(2) Each man is to entrain wearing a clean suit of underclothing plus a 2nd suit in his pack.

(3) Clean clothing will be issued up to second day before departure. This will ensure a clean change after entrain-ment.

(4) A signed voucher is to be rendered to Divisional Baths Officer of all underclothing issued to complete 2nd. suit.

15. **Regimental Equipment.**

Vehicles stores and equipment for entrainment at Antwerp will be collected as close as possible to railhead. Due consideration being given to the necessity of preserving articles from the wet. A Guard of Officer and 4 O.R.'s (to be detailed later). will remain with this equipment. and accompany it to Antwerp. When this is embarked,the Guard will be despatched by the Base Commandant to rejoin Unit in the U.K. This Guard must carefully ensure that the Regimental equipment is kept together throughout. A list of packages will be forwarded in triplicate to Div.Q.

NOTE:- Private stores. Any requisitioned articles or un-authorised are not be sent with Regimental Equipment.Any Stores in excess of A.F.G.1098 are all to be confiscated.

16. **REQUISITIONED STORES.**

All requisitioned stores of every kind including furniture pianos,mess equipment will be handed in to the local Burgomister and a detailed receipt obtained in triplicate

17. Requisitioned Stores Cont.

(1) The O.C. Unit will draw up lists showing all stores and material which have been obtained by requisition and stores and material still on charge or in possession of Unit.

(2) The lists under para.1.will be drawn up in accordance with the attached pro-forma. The list being compiled in triplicate.

(3) Prior to a Unit departing all items enumerated in the return referred to in para 1.will be handed in to the local Burgomeister will will be required to receipt these lists in triplicate. One copy will be retained by the O.C.Unit.One copy will be retained by the local burgomeister and one copy will be sent direct to branch requisition Officer G.H.Q. who will check it with the copies of the requisitioned receipt notes in his possession.

(4) Prior to any Unit leaving the Army of the Rhine, the O.C. that Unit will forward a certificate through the usual chanells to G.H.Q. that no requisitioned stores or material are being taken out of Germany either as part of his Unit's equipment or by any officer or man of his Unit. This is addition to the certificate which refers to British Stores.

(5) Arrangements will be made by sub-area commandants with the local burgomeister as to the accomodation for the storing of returned requisitioned stores etc., NOTE:- It is to be clearly understood that all furniture and other stores which have been requisitioned for officers and messes will be dealt with in accordance with the foregoing instructions.

(6) It is most important that the lists referred to in para 1.shal accurately compiled as they will at a later date be essential for coming to a final settlement of the cost of the Army of Occupation.

17. Ammunition.

All Field and H.T.Echelon will move empty.
All ammunition will be returned into depots less S.A.A. 60 rounds carried on the man and the equipment S.A.A. for Lewis Guns which will go with guns on personnel trains.(L.G.Limbers will proceed with regimentall equipment.

Bombs and Grenades.

Will be dedetonated and made safe for Transport. A Certificate to that effect will accompany each consignment. The work of dedetonating will be carried out near a pit so that the bomb may be thrown in if necessary.

Grenades will be packed and transported in their boxes and not in bags or buckets. Smoke and incend iary ammunition including phosphorus grenades should be packed and transported seperately.

Small arms grenades and T.M.ammunition will be returned to the nearest railhead which in the case of the 1V corps is VOCHEM. Date on which handing in will be commenced will be notified later. Units will commence to deliver the day after the date allocated to the previous Unit for completion.

18. H.Q. Cars.
========

 H.Q. cars will be handed in to the Military Governor.

19. Canteens.
========

 All canteens and outstanding accounts og any kind are to be settled before departure.

20. Rear Parties.
================

 The Battalion may if necessary on application to Div.H.Q. leave a rear party to clean up vacated billets. Such a party must be left in charge of an officer. All efforts will be made to void the necessity of a rear party.

21. Field Dressing.
================

 Field Dressings withdrawn under D.R.O. 3269 will be reissued to every Officer and O.R. before entrainment.

22. Pay.
=====

 In connection with the recall of men at present detached from their Units. O.C. detachments will complete A.F.O. 1809 a. showing approximate balances, rate of pay.and date to which paid and rationed. The man taking this form to the O.C. of this mans permanent Unit who will take the man on pay from the information derived therfrom in his own pay and loss book.
(2) On Units leaving for England the Imprest holder will complete his P.& M. book to the date proceeding onbarkation. The book and vouchers in support thereof,will be forwarded to the Command Paymaster. Cologne. before embarkation.
(3) Balances of cash must be refunded to the Field Cashier before leaving the Area, if not possible to the Cashier at the port of embarkation.
(4) O.C.Companies will submit a roll of Officers and N.C.O's who will embark with Coy.2 days before onbarkation. O.C.Coys. are responsible that all A.B. 64's have been sent to Command paymaster.
(5) A.E. 3447. to be submitted as usual for each Officer up to and inclusive of days if onbarkation.
    Before
(6) A. B. 64's of men on leave on England and who rejoin there must be collected and sent to Fixed Centre Paymaster.in England.

9 781474 507639